Discover
THE FRUIT
OF THE SPIRIT

by
Edith Bajema

FAITH
ALIVE®
Christian Resources

Grand Rapids, Michigan

*The fruit of the Spirit is love, joy, peace, patience, kindness,
goodness, faithfulness, gentleness and self-control.*

Galatians 5:22-23

Discover Your Bible series. *Discover the Fruit of the Spirit* (Study Guide),
© 2004 by Faith Alive Christian Resources, 1700 28th Street SE, Grand
Rapids, MI 49508-1407. All rights reserved. With the exception of brief
excerpts for review purposes, no part of this book may be reproduced in
any manner whatsoever without written permission from the publisher.
Printed in the United States of America.

We welcome your comments. Call us at 1-800-333-8300 or e-mail us at
editors@faithaliveresources.org.

ISBN 978-1-59255-207-8

10 9 8 7 6

Contents

How to Study

The questions in this study booklet will help you discover for yourself what the Bible says. This is inductive Bible study—in which you will discover the message for yourself.

Questions are the key to inductive Bible study. Through questions you search for the writers' thoughts and ideas. The questions in this booklet are designed to help you in your quest for answers. You can and should ask your own questions too. The Bible comes alive with meaning for many people as they discover the exciting truths it contains. Our hope and prayer is that this booklet will help the Bible come alive for you.

The questions in this study are designed to be used with the New International Version of the Bible, but other translations can also be used.

Step 1. Read each Bible passage several times. Allow the ideas to sink in. Think about their meaning. Ask questions about the passage.

Step 2. Answer the questions, drawing your answers from the passage. Remember that the purpose of the study is to discover what the Bible says. Write your answers in your own words. If you use Bible study aids such as commentaries or Bible handbooks, do so only after completing your own personal study.

Step 3. Apply the Bible's message to your own life. Ask,

- What is this passage saying to me?
- How does it challenge me? Comfort me? Encourage me?
- Is there a promise I should claim? A warning I should heed?
- For what can I give thanks?

If you sense God speaking to you in some way, respond to God in a personal prayer.

Step 4. Share your thoughts with someone else if possible. This will be easiest if you are part of a Bible study group that meets regularly to share discoveries and discuss questions.

If you would like to learn of a study group in your area or would like information on training to start a small group Bible study,

- call toll-free 1-888-644-0814, e-mail smallgroups@crcna.org, or visit www.smallgroupministries.org

- call toll-free 1-800-333-8300 or visit www.FaithAliveResources.org (to order materials)

Introduction

Everyone wants a fruitful life. No one wants to be like a dry, withered branch that gets cut off and thrown away. People want to be productive, vibrant, enjoying a life filled with purpose and meaning.

The Scriptures tell us the secret to the fruitful life. It's a purpose-filled life that brings blessing to others. It's a life filled with qualities that draw others—qualities like love and gentleness, peace and goodness, kindness and self-control.

But we can't produce the fruitful life on our own. We are like branches on a vine, depending wholly on the vine to supply the life flowing through us, making it possible for fruit to grow. And that life-giving vine is Jesus.

The secret to the fruitful life is in our relationship with Jesus. Our closeness to him—or our lack of it—will directly affect how well we bear fruit for him in our lives. And our openness to his Spirit's work in us—or our lack of it—will directly affect how fully our Lord's character forms within us. That character, reflecting the inner nature of God, is the fruit of the Spirit growing in us.

And what fruit it is! Nothing can compare to the beauty of this fruit that displays the very character of God:

- love that doesn't quit, that keeps giving when others have given up
- joy that fills the heart even in the most desperate circumstances
- peace that surpasses our ability to understand
- patience that endures, trusting in God's wisdom and timing
- compassionate kindness for others in their weakness
- genuine goodness that reveals the holiness of God
- faithfulness that stands firm and even grows stronger through testing (temptation) and fierce trial
- gentle strength that makes even the weakest and most insecure feel loved and safe
- self-control so disciplined that it guides us to do what is right

If you're looking for this kind of fruit in your life, this study based on Galatians 5:22-23 and other Scriptures is meant for you. Discover how the fruit of the Spirit can grow in you so that you can live the fruitful, free life God intends for us all.

Glossary of Terms

Abraham (also called Abram)—the father of the Israelite nation, called by God to leave his homeland and follow in faith to the land God promised to show him (Gen. 11:26-25:10). He is called "the father of all who believe" (Rom. 4:11; see Gal. 3:29).

apostle—one who is sent to bring the good news message of Jesus Christ as Savior. This term is usually used to refer only to those who were witnesses of the resurrected Jesus (1 Cor. 15:3-11).

atoning sacrifice—refers to *atonement,* which means "to cover over"; a sacrifice that made amends for wrongdoing (Lev. 16). By dying in our place to pay the penalty for sin, Jesus was the "atoning sacrifice for our sins" (1 John 2:2; 4:10).

blaspheme—to scoff at or revile the name of God.

Counselor—see **Holy Spirit**

cross—a torturous instrument of execution used by the Roman Empire in the days of the early church. Jesus was crucified on a cross made from a wooden crossbeam positioned on a pole with space above his head to hang a sign that read, "THIS IS THE KING OF THE JEWS" (Luke 23:38).

eternal life—the state of being forgiven and receiving new life as a child of God. This new life begins when one receives Christ by faith as Savior and Lord (2 Cor. 5:17). Having eternal life does not mean believers will not suffer physical death, but they will enjoy fellowship forever with God in this life and after death—and completely when their souls reunite with their resurrected bodies after Jesus returns and they live with God in the new heaven and new earth (1 Pet. 1:3-9; Rev. 21:1-4).

faith—"being sure of what we hope for and certain of what we do not see" (Heb. 11:1). True faith consists of accepting as true all that God has revealed in the Bible and being confident that all one's sins are forgiven through Christ's **atoning sacrifice.**

fear (of the Lord)—respectful awe of God's power and holiness, combined with love for God and obedience to God's will.

grace—God's kindness, undeserved favor, and forgiving love, won for believers through Christ's death in their place.

Holy Spirit—The Holy Spirit is God, just as God the Father and God the Son (Jesus Christ) are God. They are three persons in one being. Now that Jesus has died for our sins, conquered death, and ascended to heaven to rule at the Father's right hand, the Holy Spirit comes to live in our hearts to guide us and shape us to become like Jesus (2 Cor. 3:18; Eph. 1:3-23). God's Spirit, whom Jesus calls "the Counselor" in John 14:16, supplies us with the mind, heart, and power of God to produce in us the character of God, described in Galatians 5:22-23 as the fruit of the Spirit.

holy—set apart in a special way to bring glory to God; refers to being (declared) perfect in purity, goodness, righteousness.

hope—in combination with faith this means looking ahead in solid trust to the fulfillment of all God's promises (see Heb. 11:1).

humility—the state of humbling oneself to serve God in obedience and gratitude in response to God's salvation in Christ (see Phil. 2:1-13).

Isaac—son of Abraham and father of Jacob; Isaac was the son whom God promised to Abraham and Sarah in their old age.

Jacob—the son of Isaac who wrestled with God and was renamed Israel (Gen. 32:28); his twelve sons became the fathers of the twelve tribes of Israel (Gen. 49:1-28).

justified—declared righteous (right with God) through faith in Jesus Christ, who met the law's just demands by becoming the **atoning sacrifice** for our sins.

law—God's standard for holy living, summarized in the Ten Commandments (Ex. 20:1-17; Deut. 5:6-21) and in various other passages (see Mic. 6:8; Matt. 22:37-40).

mercy—this term is often used to describe showing kindness to someone in distress. To be more precise, it refers to showing leniency by holding back punishment even if justice calls for it.

Noah—builder of the ark that saved his family and all kinds of land animals from the worldwide punishment of sin in the Great Flood (Gen. 6-9).

prophecy, prophet—message or messenger sent by God to speak to God's people; this gift or role sometimes includes foretelling future events that God wants people to know about.

righteous, righteousness—being right with God, perfectly conformed to God's will and free from any guilt or sin. God regards believers as righteous through faith in Christ as our one Savior from sin. Righteousness relates to goodness as a quality of the fruit of the Spirit because it means doing what is right and good in all situations, as Jesus did.

salvation—freedom from death and from punishment for sin. God gives salvation to all who repent and confess their sins and believe in Jesus as Savior and Lord.

Sarah—wife of Abraham, mother of Isaac. She was far past childbearing age when she gave birth to Isaac, the child promised to her and Abraham (Gen. 18:1-15; 21:1-7).

sin offering—an offering made to atone for sin (Lev. 16); see **atoning sacrifice**.

sinful nature—the polluted, destructive nature we are born with because of human sin. The sinful nature enslaves us to be disobedient and rebellious toward God, and the only way to be rid of it is to put it to death by the power of the Holy Spirit living in us.

sons of God, sonship—being a son of God or having sonship refers to being a child of God (whether we are male or female) and thus enjoying the privilege of inheriting the salvation bought for us by our Lord, Savior, and Brother, Jesus, the Son of God. In biblical times (and in some cultures still today) only sons received a portion of the family inheritance.

tongues (speaking in tongues)—a gift of the Spirit in which a person speaks languages she or he has not learned before. The apostles spoke in various known tongues on the day of Pentecost, when the Holy Spirit was poured out on all believers (Acts 2:1-11), and other believers have spoken in "tongues of angels" (1 Cor. 13:1). The Bible cautions that the gift of tongues may be used in worship only if someone is available to interpret "for the strengthening of the church" (1 Cor. 14:26-28).

transgression—sin; refers to crossing over a line or boundary set by God for obedience.

Lesson 2
1 Corinthians 12:27-13:7; 1 John 4:7-12

Love—The Most Excellent Way

Introductory Notes

If there's one word that describes the magnificent jewel of the fruit of the Spirit, it is *love*. All the facets of this jewel are the interrelated pieces of the splendor of love: joy, peace, patience, kindness, goodness, and so on. Each is one of the many faces of love, one of the many ways in which love makes itself known.

In a comprehensive sense, love *is* the fruit of the Spirit. The other qualities we'll be exploring in these lessons are all contained in love and find their roots in love.

This lesson helps us discover the essence of love, which is the heart of God. It highlights the extremes to which love will go, its amazing endurance, its unfathomable patience, peace, faithfulness, and more. The standard of love in Scripture is nothing less than the love of God, revealed in the sacrifice of his own Son, Jesus, for our sake.

1. *1 Corinthians 12:27-31*

   a. What gifts and abilities has God given the body of Christ, the church? Why?

   b. What does the writer, Paul, want his readers to desire?

2. *1 Corinthians 13:1-3*

   a. What four gifts are mentioned in these verses?

   b. What happens when these gifts are used without love?

3. *1 Corinthians 13:4-7*

   a. What does love not consist of, according to these verses?

   b. What positive qualities describe love?

   c. What strikes you about this description of love? How easy is it to truly love others?

4. *1 John 4:7-10*

   a. Where does love come from?

b.   How has God shown love?

c.   Compare God's love with the description of love in
     1 Corinthians 13:4-7.

5.   *1 John 4:11-12*

a.   What standard of love is set for the believer?

b.   In what way are believers able to complete God's love?

Question for Reflection

What have you learned in this lesson about love as the fruit of the
Spirit? About yourself? About God?

Lesson 3

Psalm 126:3; 1 Peter 1:3-9; 1 Thessalonians 5:16; Habakkuk 3:17-19

Joy—The Lord Has Done Great Things for Us!

Introductory Notes

Joy often seems like one of the most elusive qualities in human life. For many people, the feeling of joy is like a brief gleam of sunlight that suddenly brightens things and is soon gone. Yet joy is irresistible, and people long to feel it more often. We tend to seek it in wealth, possessions, our work, relationships, our reputation, thrills, vacations, and other experiences. No matter what we try, though, it seems that this long-sought treasure never lasts.

But this idea of joy is probably better described as *happiness,* a word that has its roots in *hap,* meaning "chance" (as in *happenstance*). We are delighted by good fortune, by some surprising good news, by something that has worked out in our favor. Such fortunate events bring us feelings of happiness, which we often call joy.

The joy that the Bible speaks of, however—the joy of the Lord—is something different. As an underlying theme in Scripture, joy is linked closely to the good news of God's love for us in Jesus. Joy is not "here today, gone tomorrow." It's rock-solid, a gift of God that doesn't depend on circumstances.

1. *Psalm 126:3*

    a. What is the basis for joy, according to the psalmist?

    b. Reflect on something God has done for you or for someone you know. How did that make you feel?

2. *1 Peter 1:3-5*

    a.   On what note does the writer open these verses?

    b.   What has God done for believers in Christ?

    c.   What do you think "living hope" refers to? What made this hope possible?

    d.   What inheritance can those who love God look forward to?

3. *1 Peter 1:6-7*

    a.   What obstacles can tend to get in the way of joy?

    b.   How might even these obstacles result in joy?

4. *1 Peter 1:8-9*

    a. What kind of relationship does Peter describe?

    b. How are faith and joy related?

5. *1 Thessalonians 5:16; Habakkuk 3:17-19*

    a. How is it possible to be joyful at all times?

    b. What does Habakkuk teach us about joy?

Questions for Reflection

    a. What have you learned about true joy in these passages?

    b. What things might you do to help your joy grow?

Lesson 4
John 14:25-27; Philippians 4:6-7; Isaiah 26:3-4

Peace Beyond Understanding

Introductory Notes

Peace—a calm confidence in the midst of stress, a sense of assurance and contentment in hard times or crises. Who would not long for such a gift? Our hectic lives are often filled with anxiety and our spirits drained by worry.

Think back on times of trouble or crisis in your life. Did you have a sense of inner peace at such times? Why or why not? As you read through the Scriptures for this lesson, you'll see what made—or could have made—a difference in your anxiety level. Was prayer a part of your walk with the Spirit at that time?

As you prepare to study this lesson and aim to apply it to your everyday living, ask God to fill your heart with the wonderful gift of peace that's available as part of our faith-filled walking "in step with the Spirit" (Gal. 5:25).

1. *John 14:25-26*

    a. What is the role of the Holy Spirit in the believer's life?

    b. What comfort does the Spirit give Jesus' followers?

2. *John 14:27*

    a. Where does true peace come from, according to Jesus?

b.   What do you think is the world's idea of peace?

3. *Philippians 4:6*
    a.   What does this passage say about anxiety?

    b.   What should we do if we feel anxious?

    c.   What makes prayer so effective in stressful or uncertain situations?

4. *Philippians 4:7*
    a.   What do we receive when we bring our requests to God?

    b.   In what way does this peace go beyond human understanding?

c.   What happens to the heart and mind through prayer?

5.   *Isaiah 26:3-4*

a.   What is the relationship between peace and trust?

b.   Why is trust in God well-founded?

Question for Reflection

What have you learned in this lesson about peace and how it can grow in your life?

Lesson 5

Psalm 40:1-3; James 5:10-11; 1 Timothy 1:12-17

Patience—Training Toward Perseverance

Introductory Notes

There's a joke about the prayer of an impatient person: "Lord, please make me more patient—and hurry up about it!"

On a more serious note, that's one prayer my husband says he doesn't dare to pray, because he knows God could answer it with trials that would test his patience to the limits.

The difficult thing about patience is that it generally grows by our being stretched and pushed beyond what we think we can endure. This happens in big ways and in small ways. As we "keep in step with the Spirit" (Gal. 5:25), we grow in patience through testing that makes us rely again and again on God's timing and strength. And not only is patience useful for believers; it is also a reflection of God's character to a world much in need of God's patient love.

1. *Psalm 40:1-3*

    a. How does the psalm writer, David, describe his situation?

    b. What did David do in this situation?

    c. What was God's response, and how did this affect David?

2. *James 5:10-11*

Prophets are men and women who speak for God. Many of ancient Israel's prophets were ridiculed and persecuted, and yet they persevered in speaking God's truth to the people.

Job was a person of great faith, whose trust in God was severely tested by Satan's attacks on his life through illness, poverty, and the loss of his children (see Job 1-2). Yet Job persevered in faith, and God restored him to health and wholeness beyond what he originally had (Job 42:7-17).

a. What kind of suffering is mentioned in these verses?

b. What is the relationship between suffering, patience, and perseverance?

c. What is the value of perseverance? How is it learned?

d. What qualities in God's character enable believers to have patience in the midst of suffering?

3. *1 Timothy 1:12-17*

a. What kind of person was Paul before he was "shown mercy"?

b. How did God treat Paul? Why?

c. What was the effect of God's patience on Paul's heart?

d. What example does this set for others?

Questions for Reflection

a. Why might someone be hesitant to pray, "Lord, make me a more patient person?"

b. How is faith essential to the practice of patience?

Lesson 6

Ephesians 2:4-9; Titus 3:3-7; Luke 6:35-36;
Ephesians 4:32; Ephesians 4:2; Philippians 4:5

Kindness and Gentleness— The Incomparable Riches of Grace

Introductory Notes

Ephesians 2 gives us some fascinating snapshots of God's character: "great love," "rich in mercy," "made us alive," "grace," "raised us up," "seated us with [Christ]," "incomparable riches," "kindness," "gift of God." These words and phrases help us glimpse God's heart and actions.

It's almost too much for us to take in. Who could love human beings so much? After all, we are sinners—and yet God still values us.

God's Spirit, working through Scripture, transforms our ideas of who God is, and discovering the truth about God changes us as well. Looking at God's kindness, we become kinder. Looking at God's wealth of mercy and grace enriches our own small ability to be merciful and gracious to each other. Seeing God's gentleness with us weak sinners, we begin to treat others more gently.

1. *Ephesians 2:4-9*

    a. What great act of kindness did God do for us in Christ Jesus? (See also Rom. 5:8.)

    b. What motivated God's kindness to us?

    c. Make a list of all the good things in this passage that show God's kindness.

2. *Titus 3:3-7*

    a.   What kind of people did God show kindness to?

    b.   What is the role of the Holy Spirit in all this?

    c.   How does God's kindness in Jesus Christ bring us hope?

3. *Luke 6:35-36*

    a.   Why does Jesus tell his followers to show kindness to their enemies?

    b.   What are some ways believers can do this?

4. *Ephesians 4:32*

    a.   How are believers to treat each other?

b.   What is the basis for such kindness?

5. *Ephesians 4:2; Philippians 4:5*
    a.   How is gentleness related to humility and patience?

    b.   What does gentleness communicate to others?

Questions for Reflection
    a.   In what relationships would you like to be able to grow in kindness and gentleness?

    b.   What is the best way to go about doing this?

Lesson 7
Luke 6:43-45; Psalm 37:3-6; Proverbs 14:22;
Ephesians 5:8-10; Matthew 5:16

Goodness—Living in the Light

Introductory Notes

This lesson speaks of the goodness that grows in our lives as a quality of the fruit of the Spirit, a by-product of the believer's closeness with God. This goodness is not an attempt to earn salvation but rather a sign of having spiritual health because we are saved in Christ and the Spirit is working in us.

The Scripture passages for this lesson make a clear distinction between goodness and evil. The Bible uses many different pictures for this distinction: light versus darkness, good fruit versus bad, the right path versus the wrong, true riches versus false. So as we examine the quality of goodness, we'll be looking again at the believer's struggle to choose good over evil as the Holy Spirit works in the believer's heart to fight against the sinful nature (Gal. 5:17; see Rom. 7:15-25).

1. *Luke 6:43-45*

    a.   How does Jesus relate fruit-bearing trees to people?

    b.   What do a person's actions have to do with his or her heart?

2. *Psalm 37:3-6*

    a.   Why might goodness require trust in God?

b.   How does God treat those who delight in him?

c.   What does God promise here for the person who acts in righteousness (goodness)?

3.   *Proverbs 14:22*

a.   What happens to the path of the person who plots evil or disobeys God? The person who plans good?

b.   How is goodness related to love and faithfulness?

4.   *Ephesians 5:8-10*

a.   What change takes place in us when we follow Christ?

b.   How are goodness and light related?

c. What does goodness have to do with pleasing the Lord?

5. *Matthew 5:16*
    a. What is the ultimate purpose of the believer's goodness?

    b. How does the idea of goodness and light in this verse relate to Ephesians 5:8-10?

Questions for Reflection
    a. How would you like to see the fruit of goodness grow in your life?

    b. What can you do toward accomplishing this?

Lesson 8
Hebrews 11:1-3, 7-16; 12:1-3

Faithfulness—Living by Faith

Introductory Notes

The Bible teaches that faith involves relationship—the relationship between God and the believer. Christians believe that God is who God says he is and that God will do as he promises. Because God is faithful, because God's promises are trustworthy, because God's power is reliable and God's compassion is genuine, Christians are able to live "faith-full" lives. They can follow God's leading and be faithful to God's commands because God is faithfully at work through the Holy Spirit in their lives. The Spirit is always there to remind believers of God's faithfulness and to empower them to live faithfully for God. In turn, the faithfulness of believers reveals God's faithful character to the world. They are becoming more and more like God so that others can see in them the strength and tender faithfulness of God.

1. *Hebrews 11:1-3*

   a. How is faith described in these verses?

   b. What were the earliest believers in God commended for?

   c. What does faith in God have to do with our view of the world and of history?

2. *Hebrews 11:7*

    a. What did Noah do out of faithful obedience? (See also Gen. 6-8.)

    b. What did Noah receive as a result?

3. *Hebrews 11:8-12*

    a. What journey did Abraham make? (See also Gen. 12:1-7.) Why?

    b. What miracle happened in Abraham's old age? (See also Gen. 15:1-5; 21:1-7; Rom. 4:18-21.)

4. *Hebrews 11:13-16*

    a. What were these faithful believers looking forward to?

    b. How did this please God?

5. *Hebrews 12:1-3*

    a.   What role do heroes of the faith play for believers today?

    b.   What ultimate example of faithfulness can believers look to?

    c.   What effect does Jesus' example have?

Question for Reflection

    If you were to live a more "faith-full" life, what challenges do you think you would face?

Lesson 9

Romans 8:1-16; Galatians 5:24-25

Self-Control—Freed to Live by the Spirit

Introductory Notes

We like to think we are free to make our own choices, that we are in control of our minds and hearts, our thoughts and decisions. But self-control in our natural human state is a myth. Something has had control of us since birth: our sinful nature, as we discussed in lesson 1.

Remember how Paul describes the human condition as being enslaved to sin? In Romans 7, Paul writes of his own struggle to do what he knows is right: "I do not understand what I do. For what I want to do I do not do, but what I hate I do. . . . I have the desire to do what is good, but I cannot carry it out" (Rom. 7:15-18). Acting on his own strength, Paul had insufficient self-control to make himself do what he knew was right, or to keep from doing what he knew was wrong. Thankfully Paul explains further that there's a way out: we can be controlled by the Spirit rather than by the sinful nature. That teaching in Romans 8 provides much of the Scripture you'll be discussing in this lesson.

In Galatians 5, Paul teaches that self-control is a quality of the Spirit's work in our lives, and in connection with this, we'll look again at Galatians 5:24-25 to see what these verses teach about self-control. Self-control is not really what it sounds like; it actually involves giving over control of one's heart and thoughts to the Spirit of God—but at the same time that means being freed to live by the Spirit, as we also discussed in lesson 1. Only through the Spirit's work can we break the sinful nature's powerful hold on us. Only through the Spirit's power can we find the discipline and strength to do the good that we long to do instead of the sin that we don't want to do.

1. *Romans 8:1-4*

   a. Why are believers no longer condemned when they sin?

   b. What does this have to do with self-control, or the lack of it?

c. How did God fulfill the just demands of the law while still offering forgiveness and freedom to sinners?

2. *Romans 8:5-11*

   a. What does it mean that "the mind of sinful man is death" (v. 6)?

   b. How is life different when the mind is controlled by the Spirit?

   c. What does this teach us about self-control?

   d. In the Spirit of Christ's strength, what hope do believers have for the future?

   e. What's the outlook for people controlled by the sinful nature?

3. *Romans 8:12-16*

   a. What is expected of believers who want to live by the Spirit?

   b. To whom do believers ultimately give control of their hearts? What do they call him?

4. *Galatians 5:24-25*

   a. Compare this passage with Romans 8:12-16. What does each passage say about dealing with the sinful nature and living by the Spirit?

   b. How does this passage describe the spiritual quality of self-control?

Questions for Reflection

   a. What have you learned about self-control?

   b. What do you find challenging about keeping in step with the Spirit?

An Invitation

Listen now to what God is saying to you.

You may be aware of things in your life that keep you from coming near to God. You may have thought of God as someone who is unsympathetic, angry, and punishing. You may feel as if you don't know how to pray or how to come near to God.

"But because of his great love for us, God, who is rich in mercy, made us alive with Christ even when we were dead in transgressions—it is by grace you have been saved" (Eph. 2:4-5). Jesus, God's Son, died on the cross to save us from our sins. It doesn't matter where you come from, what you've done in the past, or what your heritage is. God has been watching over you and caring for you, drawing you closer. "And you also were included in Christ when you heard the message of truth, the gospel of your salvation" (Eph. 1:13).

Do you want to receive Jesus as your Savior and Lord? It's as simple as A-B-C:

- **A**dmit that you have sinned and that you need God's forgiveness.
- **B**elieve that God loves you and that Jesus has already paid the price for your sins.
- **C**ommit your life to God in prayer, asking God to forgive your sins, nurture you as his child, and fill you with the Holy Spirit.

Prayer of Commitment

Here is a prayer of commitment recognizing Jesus Christ as Savior. If you long to be in a loving relationship with Jesus, pray this prayer. If you have already committed your life to Jesus, use this prayer for renewal and praise.

Dear God, I come to you simply and honestly to confess that I have sinned, that sin is a part of who I am. And yet I know that you listen to sinners who are truthful before you. So I come with empty hands and heart, asking for forgiveness.

I confess that only through faith in Jesus Christ can I come to you. I confess my need for a Savior, and I thank you, Jesus, for dying on the cross to pay the price for my sins. Lord, I ask that you forgive my sins and count me among those who are righteous in your sight. Remove the guilt that accompanies sin and bring me into your presence.

Holy Spirit of God, help me to pray, and teach me to live by your Word. Faithful God, help me to serve you faithfully. Make me more and more like Jesus each day, and help me to share with others the good news of your great salvation. In Jesus' name, Amen.

Evaluation Questionnaire

DISCOVER THE FRUIT OF THE SPIRIT

As you complete this study, please fill out this questionnaire to help us evaluate the effectiveness of our materials. Please be candid. Thank you.

1. Was this a home group ___ or a church-based ___ program? What church?

2. Was the study used for
    ___ a community evangelism group?
    ___ a community faith-nurture group?
    ___ a church Bible study group?

3. How would you rate the materials?

    Study Guide
    ___ excellent ___ very good ___ good ___ fair ___ poor

    Leader Guide
    ___ excellent ___ very good ___ good ___ fair ___ poor

4. What were the strengths?

5. What were the weaknesses?

6. What would you suggest to improve the material?

7. In general, what was the experience of your group?

Your name (optional) _____

Address _____

_____

8. Other comments:

(Please fold, tape, stamp, and mail. Thank you.)

Faith Alive Christian Resources
1700 28th Street SE
Grand Rapids, MI 49508-1407